FAMILY LEARNING

from Dorling Kindersley

The Family Learning mission is to support the concept of the home as a centre of learning and to help families develop independent learning skills to last a lifetime.

For my daughter, Kirsten Margaret Baumgartner

Art Editors   Sarah Stanley and Mark Regardsoe
Editor   Nicholas Turpin
Senior Editor   Marie Greenwood
Managing Art Editor   Jacquie Gulliver
Production   Steve Lang
DTP Designer   Kim Browne

Published by Family Learning

Dorling Kindersley registered offices:
9 Henrietta Street, London WC2E 8PS

VISIT US ON THE WORLD WIDE WEB at:
http://www.dk.com

ISBN: 0-7513-7165-3

Colour reproduction by GRB Editrice, Italy
Printed in Belgium

A CIP catalogue record for this book is available from the British Library.

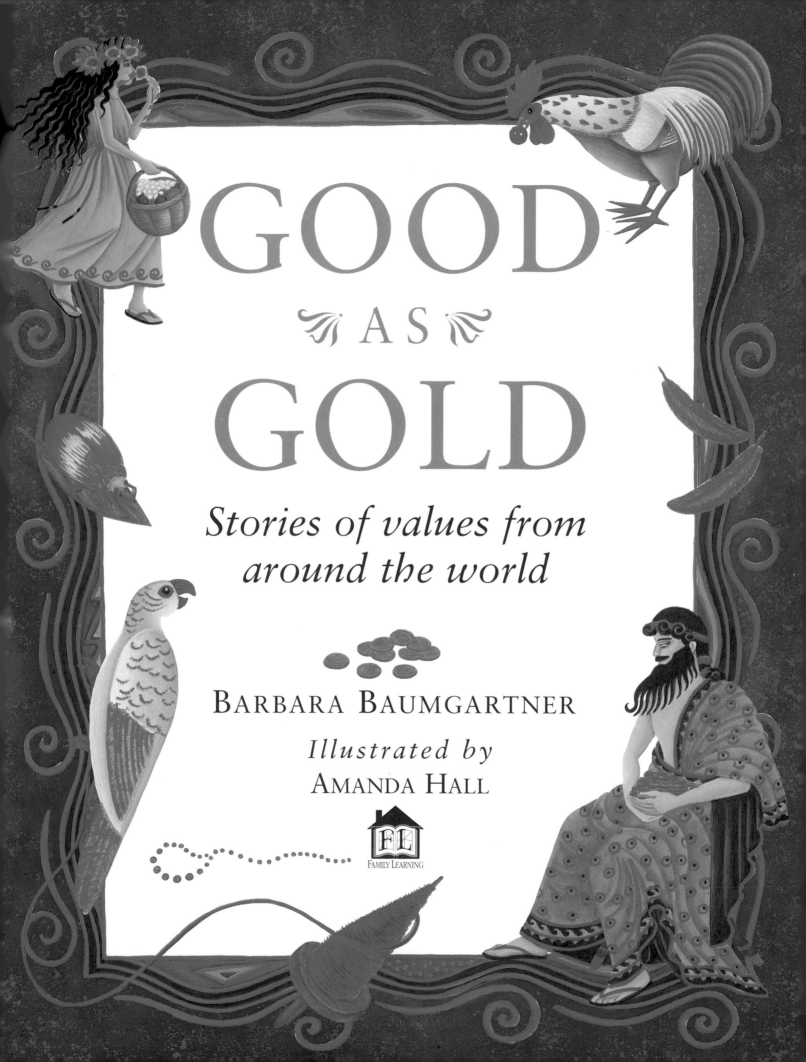

GOOD

❧ AS ❧

GOLD

*Stories of values from
around the world*

BARBARA BAUMGARTNER

Illustrated by
AMANDA HALL

FL
FAMILY LEARNING

Introduction

A note for parents and teachers

MUCH OF OUR GROWING UP involves learning from our own mistakes and adventures. Stories give us vicarious experiences from which we can discover even more. Occasionally after I tell children a story, I ask an open-ended question, such as "I wonder what part of the story is most important." This gives the children a chance to reflect on the story and tell me what is meaningful for each of them.

Sometimes children ask, "What is the *moral* of that story?" I like to turn the question back to them by asking: "What do *you* think is the moral of the story?" Usually when I do that, the children identify several lessons in a tale.

In this collection, a moral is written at the end of each story. But it is not necessary to read the moral each time you read the story, and, if you ask the children, you'll find out what the story means to them.

Contents

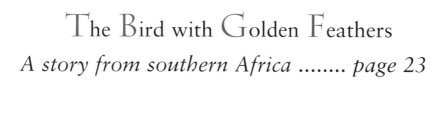

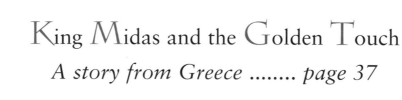

The Rooster
and the Golden Button

LONG AGO there was a woman who was very poor. She had one skinny rooster. Every day the Little Rooster ran out of the gate to scratch in the dirt road for bugs and worms.

One day, when the Little Rooster was scratching in the dirt, he found a golden button. He was so excited! He would take it to the woman, and she could use it to buy food.

Now just at that moment, the Sultan – the mean-tempered ruler of that land – came walking down the road.

He was wearing a turban on his head, a fancy shirt, and baggy trousers.

When he saw the Rooster holding the golden button in his beak, the Sultan snatched the golden button, and stuffed it into his pocket – oops!

Not that pocket.
That was the one with the hole in it.
He stuffed the button into the *other* pocket.
The Little Rooster crowed:

"Cock-a-doodle-dooo!

That's **my** button!
Give me back my golden button!"
The cruel Sultan pretended he
didn't hear the Little Rooster.
He hurried back to his castle.

The Little Rooster followed the Sultan to his castle. He perched on the window-sill and he crowed:

"Cock-a-doodle-dooo!

That's **my** button!
Give me back my golden button!"
The Sultan said, "Guards, take that Little Rooster and throw him into the well!"
The guards grabbed the Little Rooster and threw him into the well.
The Little Rooster was scared! But he sang out:
"Come my empty stomach, drink up all the water."
His empty stomach drank up all the water.
Then the Little Rooster flew back to the Sultan's window.
He crowed:

"Cock-a-doodle-dooo!

That's **my** button!
Give me back my golden button!"
The Sultan said, "Guards, take that
Little Rooster and throw him into the fire!"
The guards grabbed the Little Rooster
and tossed him into the fire.
The Little Rooster was scared!
But he sang out:
    "Come my full stomach,
    give up all the water."
All the water came pouring out of
the Little Rooster's mouth, and put
out the fire.

Then the Little Rooster flew back to the Sultan's window. He crowed:

"Cock-a-doodle-dooo!

That's **my** button! Give me back my golden button!" The Sultan said, "Guards, take that Little Rooster and throw him into the beehive."

The guards grabbed the Little Rooster and threw him into the beehive. The Little Rooster was scared! But he sang out, "Come, my empty stomach, eat up all the bees."

His empty stomach ate up all the bees. Then the Little Rooster flew back to the Sultan's window. He crowed:

"Cock-a-doodle-dooo!

That's **my** button! Give me back my golden button!"

The Sultan was *so* angry. He said, "Little Rooster, I cannot get rid of you, so I will stuff you into my pocket." But the Sultan stuffed the Little Rooster into the wrong pocket – the one with the hole! The Little Rooster stuck his beak through the hole and sang out:

"Come my full stomach, give up all the bees!"

The bees flew out of the Rooster's mouth and began stinging the Sultan's legs.

The Sultan jumped up and down, shouting, "Guards, cut open my trousers, and let out the bees!"

When the bees had flown away, the Sultan took the rooster out of one pocket, and the golden button out of the other.

"Here," he said, "take your golden button!"

The Little Rooster crowed:

"Cock-a-doodle-dooo!

Thank you for my button!"

Then he hurried home with the button in his beak. He gave it to the woman, and she used the golden button to buy food and warm clothes, enough to last for a long time.

WHEN YOU ARE IN DIFFICULTY, USE YOUR WITS.

Why the Beetle
has a Gold Coat

LONG AGO when animals talked like people, the beetles in Brazil had ordinary, plain brown coats. One day a brown beetle was crawling along a wall. A brown paca ran by and called out, "You are so slow!" The paca raced to the end of the wall, then ran back to the beetle. "I bet you would like to run that fast!"

The little beetle said politely, "Yes, Mr Paca, you do run fast."

A parrot had heard their conversation. He preened his green and gold feathers. Then he said to the paca, "How would you like to race the beetle? I will ask the tailor bird to make a bright-coloured coat for the winner of the race."

The paca looked over his shoulders
at his brown fur with a few white spots.
He said, "I would like a coat like the
jaguar's, yellow with black spots."
He was sure he would
win the race.

The parrot nodded towards the palm tree growing at the top of the hill. "That tree will be the goal. Whoever gets there first will win a new coat!"

The parrot signalled for the race to begin. Then he flew to the top of the palm tree.

The paca began to run fast. After a while he was out of breath. He stopped to rest and to drink some water. "There's no need to hurry," he said to himself. "That little beetle is so slow!"

After a short rest, the paca began to run again. He ran and ran until he had reached the palm tree. But when he got there, he saw that the little brown beetle was already sitting on a palm branch next to the parrot.

The paca said, "Beetle, how did you run so fast?"

The beetle opened her wings and fluttered them in the sunlight. "No one said that I had to *run* to win the race. So I flew."

The paca groaned, "I did not know that you could fly!"

The parrot said, "After this, do not judge anyone by looks alone. You can never tell what hidden talents another creature may have."

Then the parrot turned to the little beetle, "What colour would you like for your new coat?"

The beetle looked at the golden sunshine on the green leaves. She admired the green and gold feathers of the parrot. Then she said, "I would like a coat of green and gold."

That is why the Brazilian beetle wears a coat of green and gold, while the paca is still brown.

 Do not judge by looks alone. You can never tell what hidden talents another may have.

Maria

and the Stingy Baker

L ONG AGO in Peru there was a young woman named Maria who lived near the baker's house. Maria was very poor. She earned her food by washing clothes for other people in the village. They would pay her with a basket of eggs or some vegetables from their gardens.

Each morning Maria got up early and washed clothes. While she was hanging them outside to dry, she looked over at the window of the baker's house. Already he had loaves of bread cooling at his open window. Maria loved the wonderful smell of fresh-baked bread that came from the baker's house. She would imagine that she was a queen and that the rolls and loaves of bread would soon be hers to eat.

When she walked by the baker's house, Maria sometimes called out, "Thank you, Baker. I love the smell of your delicious bread."

But the baker was a stingy fellow.

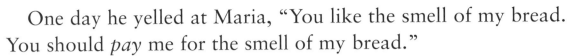

One day he yelled at Maria, "You like the smell of my bread. You should *pay* me for the smell of my bread."

Maria laughed. "Oh, Baker, that would be silly. I shouldn't have to pay you for the *smell* of your bread."

Then the baker roared, "Oh, yes you should. Every morning I get up early. I mix the flour and yeast, the butter and salt. I stir and knead the dough till my arms ache. You enjoy the smell of my bread and don't give me anything in return. You should pay me ten pieces of gold each month!"

When the neighbours overheard the conversation between Maria and the baker, they began to laugh and joke among themselves.

Did you hear what that baker wants to do? He wants Maria to pay him because she enjoys the smell of his fresh-baked bread!

The baker became more and more annoyed. It seemed to him that everyone was laughing at him. Finally one afternoon the baker went to see the judge, who was well-known for her wise decisions. He complained to the judge, and the next morning there was a notice in the town square:

THE JUDGE

will hear the case between

the BAKER and MARIA.

They must come to the court in three days.

MARIA must bring a bag containing

ten gold coins.

Maria was scared. She did not have ten gold coins. She did not have *one* gold coin. Maria didn't know what to do. People gave her food in exchange for doing their laundry. A gold coin was worth so much, that Maria would have to wash clothes for one person for a whole year in order to earn one gold coin. But that afternoon when she took the clean, dry laundry to the house of the old woman who lived on the hill, the woman said, "Maria, I will give you a gold coin to take to court." Each time she went to one of her regular customers to pick up laundry or return it, that person gave her a gold coin. She promised each person she would repay them as soon as possible.

By the morning of the third day, Maria had ten gold coins. She tied them in the corner of her scarf, and she walked to court.

Everyone in the village was gathered in the courtroom to hear the trial between Maria and the baker. The judge called the court to order. Then she asked the baker to state his case.

The stingy baker spoke. "Every morning I get up early to start baking bread. I mix the flour and yeast, the butter and salt. I stir and knead the dough till my arms ache. Maria enjoys the smell of my bread, but she never gives me anything in return. She should pay me ten pieces of gold each month!"

Next the judge called Maria forward. "Maria," she said, "Is it true that you smell the baker's bread every morning?"

"Yes, I do," said Maria.

"Is it true that you enjoy the smell of the baker's bread?"

"Yes, I do," said Maria.

"Did you bring ten pieces of gold with you today?"

"Yes, I did," said Maria, "but I should not have to pay the baker for the *smell* of his bread. If I *ate* some of his bread, then I should have to pay him."

The judge said, "I will decide that later. Right now, Maria, I would like you to shake the ten gold coins that you brought with you."

Maria held out the corner of her scarf in which she had tied the coins. She shook the bundle, and everyone in the courtroom could hear the coins jingling.

The judge said, "Everyone leave the courtroom for fifteen minutes. When you come back, I will announce my decision."

Maria went outside. The baker was standing in the middle of the town square, gleefully rubbing his hands together.

"I know the judge is going to award me the ten gold coins," he said. Other villagers were talking among themselves, trying to guess what the judge would decide.

When all the people had returned to the courtroom, the judge announced her decision: "Maria has enjoyed the smell of your bread. You have enjoyed the sound of her money. I pronounce this a fair exchange.

Case dismissed!"

TRADES AND EXCHANGES
MUST BE FAIR.

The Bird
with Golden Feathers

LONG AGO in Malawi there lived a man named Kwende and his wife, Sabola. They always had to work hard. When the spring near their house dried up, Sabola had to walk a long way to get water. Every day, as Kwende set out to hunt for food, he saw a large, beautiful bird flying near the path.

One day Kwende was returning home without having caught any food. He was hungrier than usual, and suddenly remembered that he had not checked one of his traps. When he got to that trap, he saw that he had caught the beautiful bird that he had seen flying near the path.

Kwende grabbed the bird by the neck, and pulled out his knife, planning to kill it and take it home for Sabola to cook.

But the bird said to him, "Spare my life and I will repay you for your kindness."

Kwende put the knife away and looked more closely at the bird. Its feathers were the colour of gold. The bird said, "My golden feathers are magic. With them you will be able to supply all of your needs. Please release me from this trap."

Kwende thought to himself, *Is the bird trying to trick me so that he can get free? If the bird is speaking the truth, I will never again have to work so hard. But whoever heard of a bird that talked?*

He untied the thong that was cutting into the bird's leg. As Kwende watched, the bird pulled one golden feather from each wing and held them in his beak so Kwende could take them.

Then the bird told him how to use them. "As you hold the feathers in your hands, make a wish and it will come true. But I warn you, never tell anyone about the magical power of these feathers. And do not boast of your good fortune, or the power of my gift will vanish and you will be poor again."

Kwende thanked the bird, and it flew away. As he walked quickly home, Kwende held a feather in each hand and wished that he would find plenty of food when he arrived home.

When he got home, Sabola was stirring a pot of cornmeal while a pot of stew bubbled on the cooking fire. Nearby lay a pile of yams, so he knew they would have food for tomorrow. The nearby spring that had been dried up for so long, was now gushing water. Sabola would not have to trudge a long distance to bring back their water.

For days and weeks and months, Kwende and Sabola were showered with good fortune. There was always food to eat, clothes to wear, and water to drink. Kwende did no work, but lay in the shade of a tree all day. Sabola often asked him why he was not working in the garden or hunting in the forest. But he would not answer her questions.

But then Kwende became careless. He began boasting to his neighbours of his good fortune. Sabola was worried and she asked him, "Kwende, you do no work, and yet we have so much food. Are you stealing from others during the night? I will have to ask the wise woman to find out what you're hiding from me."

Kwende protested, "Sabola, do not ask the wise woman anything. She will find out about the magic golden feathers, and will try to steal them from me."

Suddenly Kwende realized that he had disobeyed the bird's warnings. He had boasted to others, and he had talked out loud about the magic feathers.

The next day when he held the two golden feathers and wished his daily wishes, nothing happened. There was no food in the cooking pots. The bubbling spring dried up. Sabola and Kwende were again poor and hungry. But this time their poverty seemed even worse after they had enjoyed wealth and plenty of food.

Once again Kwende had to go out daily to set traps and hunt for food. One day he went hunting with a neighbour who brought along his dog. They had hunted all day and caught nothing. But when they arrived at Kwende's last trap, he saw that he had captured the same golden bird.

Kwende rushed forward. "Oh golden bird, give me two of your magic feathers again, and I will release you."

The bird said, "Please spare my life a second time."

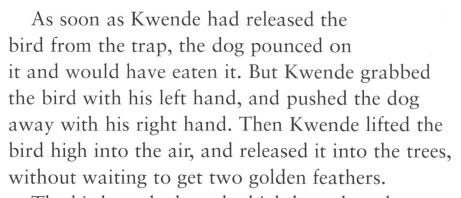

As soon as Kwende had released the bird from the trap, the dog pounced on it and would have eaten it. But Kwende grabbed the bird with his left hand, and pushed the dog away with his right hand. Then Kwende lifted the bird high into the air, and released it into the trees, without waiting to get two golden feathers.

The bird perched on the high branch and spoke again. "I hope you remember the lessons you learned when you disobeyed my warnings and my conditions. I know that you and your wife have suffered. Because you have saved my life a second time, I will give you two feathers without any conditions. Their magic will last forever."

The bird plucked one golden feather from each wing, and the feathers floated down to Kwende. Then the golden bird spread its wings and rose into the sky. Kwende never saw it again. But he and Sabola lived in comfort and in peace. He never boasted about his good fortune. But he gave thanks for it every day.

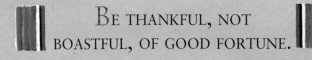

BE THANKFUL, NOT BOASTFUL, OF GOOD FORTUNE.

Rumpelstiltskin
the Gold Spinner

ONCE UPON A TIME there was a miller whose daughter was not only beautiful but also clever. One day, when the miller was boasting to his friends, he said, "My daughter is so clever that I bet she could spin straw into gold."

Now the King overheard this as he was passing by, and he ordered the miller to send his daughter to the castle the very next day.

When the girl got to the castle, the King led her into a room filled with straw. At one side of the room sat a spinning wheel and a chair. The King said, "You must spin this straw into gold by tomorrow morning."

Before the girl could utter a word of protest, the King had slammed the door and locked it. She sat down and she began to cry.

Soon she heard a voice at the window. She looked up and there was a strange-looking little man. He said, "Mistress miller, why are you crying?"

"Oh, dear," she said, "the King has asked me to spin this straw into gold by morning, and I don't know how to do it."

The little man said, "What will you give me if I spin it for you?"

She said, "I could give you my necklace."

So he took her necklace, and he sat down at the spinning wheel. As he picked up a handful of straw, he sang a song:

*♪ "Spin and hum, spin and hum,
Now the night is just begun." ♪*

As the little man sang, he spun all the straw into gold. Then he disappeared into the night.

The next morning when the King came, the sight of all that gold only made him greedier. He gave the girl food and drink. That night he took her to another room full of straw and said, "Tonight you must spin this straw into gold if you value your life."

Again he slammed the door and locked her in. The girl sat down and began to cry.

Then she heard the voice at the window, and the little man said, "What will you give me if I help you?"

"I could give you my ring," said the girl.

So the little man took the ring, and sat down at the spinning wheel. As he picked up a handful of straw, he sang:

*"Spin and hum, spin and hum,
Now the night is just half done."*

The little man worked half the night, until all the straw was spun into gold. Then he disappeared.

The next morning when the King came in and saw the room full of gold, he was very pleased. He said, "If you can spin another roomful of straw tonight, then I will have you marry my son, the Prince."

The girl did not know what to do. She was afraid that if she argued with the King, he would hurt her. So that night he again led her to a room, and locked her in. The girl sat down on a stool and began to weep.

Just then she heard the voice of the little man. "Mistress miller, what will you give me if I spin that straw into gold?"

"Oh," the girl moaned, "I have nothing left to give you."

The little man rubbed his hands together. "Promise you will give me your first-born child."

The girl gasped. But then she thought, *Who knows if I will ever have a child?* And so she promised.

The little man sat down at the spinning wheel and he picked up a handful of straw.

*"Spin and hum, spin and hum,
Soon the night will all be done."*

When the little man had spun all the straw into gold, he disappeared into the night. The next morning the King came and was pleased. He had his servants dress the miller's daughter in a wedding gown, and that day she was married to the Prince, the King's own son, and she was called Princess.

A year later, a baby boy was born to the Princess. She was so delighted with the child that she completely forgot about her promise to the little man. But one evening, the little man stood in the doorway and said, "Now, I've come for what you promised."

The Princess begged and pleaded with the little man – she would give him money or jewels if he would only let her keep the baby.

Finally he said to her, "I will give you three days to guess my name. If you guess it right, you may keep your child. But if you cannot guess my name, the child is mine!" Then he disappeared out of the door.

All the next day the Princess made lists of names. That night when the little man stood in the doorway, she said,

"Is your name Anthony? Or Benjamin? Or Steven?"

Each time he answered, "That is not my name."

The second day the Princess made lists of unusual names. When the little man came, she asked, "Is your name Mutton Bones? Or Sheep Shanks? Or String Bean?"

Each time he answered, "That is not my name."

The third day, when the Prince and Princess were eating lunch together, the Prince said, "My dear, I was out hunting yesterday and I saw the strangest thing. As I walked to the top of a hill, I happened to look down into a little hollow. In the clearing, I saw a fire burning, and a strange little man was dancing around the fire and singing,

"Today I'll bake, tomorrow I'll brew,
And then the royal son I'll claim.
Oh lucky me, for no one knows
That Rumpelstiltskin is my name."

The Princess was so astonished that she almost choked on her food, but she merely said, "What a curious thing."

That evening when the little man stood in her doorway, the Princess pretended to be trembling with fear.

"Oh dear, is your name Tom?"

"No, that is not my name!"

"Is your name Will?"

"No, that is not my name!"

"Then perhaps your name is Rumpelstiltskin!"

The little man shrieked, "Who told you that? Who told you that?" He stomped his feet in anger, then stormed out of the door.

And he was never seen again.

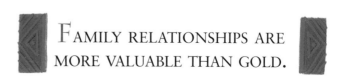

FAMILY RELATIONSHIPS ARE MORE VALUABLE THAN GOLD.

King Midas
and the Golden Touch

L ONG AGO in the country of Greece, there lived a king named Midas. He was proud of his palace and his beautiful gardens, but most of all he was proud of his seven-year-old daughter, whose name was Marigold.

King Midas was a rich man, but he was not a happy man. He longed for more gold, so that he could buy fancier foods and prettier dresses for his daughter.

Sometimes he would sit in his counting room, carefully counting out piles of gold coins, gold necklaces, and gold bracelets.

One day, when King Midas was in his counting room, his little daughter Marigold knocked on the door.

"Father," she said, "it's such a pretty day. Come and have a picnic with me in the warm, golden sun."

King Midas did not open the door, but spoke gruffly to her, "No, Marigold, I am busy right now."

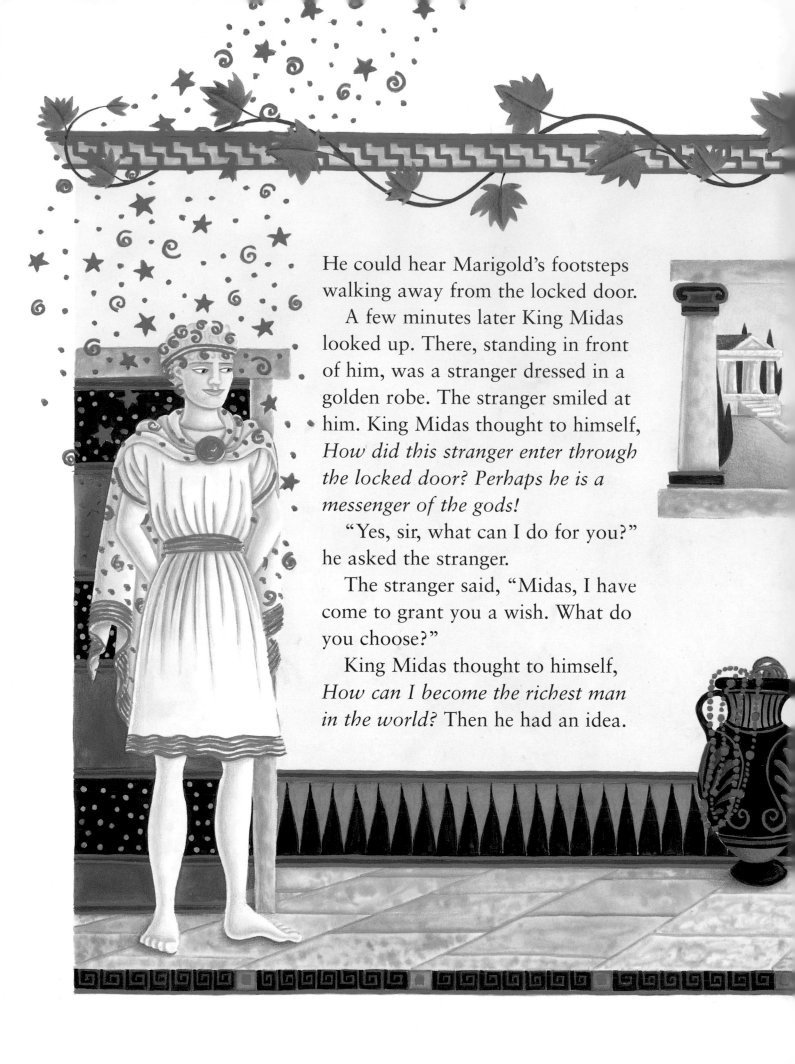

He could hear Marigold's footsteps walking away from the locked door.

A few minutes later King Midas looked up. There, standing in front of him, was a stranger dressed in a golden robe. The stranger smiled at him. King Midas thought to himself, *How did this stranger enter through the locked door? Perhaps he is a messenger of the gods!*

"Yes, sir, what can I do for you?" he asked the stranger.

The stranger said, "Midas, I have come to grant you a wish. What do you choose?"

King Midas thought to himself, *How can I become the richest man in the world?* Then he had an idea.

He said to the stranger, "I wish that everything I touch would turn to gold!"

"Ah-ha," said the stranger, "the Golden Touch. Your wish is granted. Tomorrow morning you will have the Golden Touch."

"Thank you, thank you!" said King Midas as he bowed to the stranger. When he looked up, the stranger had disappeared.

That night King Midas could hardly sleep, thinking about how rich he would be once he had the Golden Touch.

When he awoke the next morning, the sun was shining through the window. King Midas touched his blue blanket, and suddenly it shimmered with gold, but was still soft and warm.

King Midas leaped out of bed. He began running around his room, touching things to see them change to gold. He touched the chair, the bedposts, the table, and they all turned gold. As he dressed himself, all his clothes turned to gold. King Midas was so excited that he went out to his garden. He began touching all the flowers, so that the red poppies and the tall, blue flowers all glittered gold.

Then he went into his house to eat. One of the servants brought him a plate of fruit, bread, and cheese. King Midas was hungry. As he picked up the knife to slice the cheese, the knife turned to gold. He was so excited! Why now everything in this house could be gold!

But when his fingers touched the cheese, it turned to a lump of gold. Then King Midas tried to slice the bread, but it also turned to gold. He picked up an apple, and it turned to gold.

Now King Midas began to grumble to himself, "I don't see how I will stay alive if I cannot eat anything. I will starve to death in a few days!"

Just then Marigold came running into the room. She was clutching a golden flower and crying. "Father," she said, "something terrible has happened to the flowers. They have turned this nasty yellow colour and they don't smell good anymore." King Midas reached out to hug Marigold, and she turned to gold.

He was horrified. His dear daughter was a solid gold statue, with golden tears on her cheeks.

As he groaned out loud, King Midas looked up and saw the stranger who had visited him the day before. The stranger smiled at him and said, "Well, King Midas, what do you think of the Golden Touch?"

"Oh I am miserable," he said. "The Golden Touch has only brought me bad luck. I cannot eat, because everything I touch turns to gold. And now I have turned my sweet daughter Marigold into a golden statue."

"Which would you rather have," asked the stranger, "the Golden Touch or a slice of bread?"

King Midas said, "I would rather be able to eat a piece of bread than to have all the gold in the world."

"Which would you rather have," asked the stranger, "the Golden Touch or your daughter Marigold, alive and breathing as she was an hour ago?"

"No one is more dear to me than she is," said King Midas. "Yes, I would rather have her than the Golden Touch."

"You have grown wiser in one day," said the stranger. "Bathe in the river that flows past your garden. The water will cleanse you of the Golden Touch. And bring a pitcher of the water to sprinkle over your daughter."

King Midas thanked the stranger. Then he grabbed a clay pitcher, which immediately changed to gold, and hurried to the river. As he bathed in the river, his clothes turned back to their normal colour.

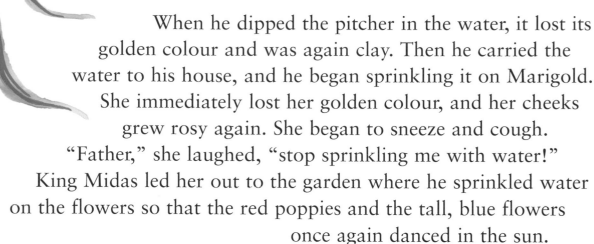

When he dipped the pitcher in the water, it lost its
golden colour and was again clay. Then he carried the
water to his house, and he began sprinkling it on Marigold.
She immediately lost her golden colour, and her cheeks
grew rosy again. She began to sneeze and cough.
"Father," she laughed, "stop sprinkling me with water!"
King Midas led her out to the garden where he sprinkled water
on the flowers so that the red poppies and the tall, blue flowers
once again danced in the sun.

GREED DESTROYS
HUMAN HAPPINESS.

Two Brothers
and the Pumpkin Seeds

LONG AGO in Korea there were two brothers: Chang, who was so stingy he would not share a piece of food with you, and Kim, who was always kind and helpful. One day the two brothers saw a young swallow fall from its nest and break its leg. Kim quickly picked up the bird and bound its leg so that the bone would heal.

Chang shouted, "Foolish! Silly! Wrapping up a bird's leg!"

Kim took the swallow into the house, and when the bird's leg healed, Kim set it free.

A few days later, the swallow returned and dropped a pumpkin seed at Kim's feet. Kim planted the pumpkin seed in a corner of the field. Every day he watered the seed and pulled up the weeds. Soon a vine began to grow, with one pumpkin growing under its leaves.

At harvest time the pumpkin had grown so big that Kim thought, *This pumpkin is too heavy to move. I will cut it open and give a piece to each family in the village.*

But when Kim cut the pumpkin open, gold coins tumbled out. So Kim shared the pumpkin and the gold coins with everyone in the village.

When Chang saw all that had happened, he decided he would like such good fortune. He found a young swallow, then cruelly broke its leg. He bound the swallow's leg with a bandage and then released the bird. A few days later, the bird returned with a pumpkin seed in its beak. Chang snatched the pumpkin seed and hurried to plant it in the field. Soon a pumpkin vine was growing.

When Chang was ready to harvest his pumpkin, he said to himself, *I will not be foolish like my brother and give away the pumpkin and its gold.*

When he cut into the pumpkin, spiders and snakes began crawling all over him. At the same time, the pumpkin vine began growing up towards the sky. Chang quickly began climbing the pumpkin vine to get away from the spiders and snakes. But when he got into the sky, the vine dried up behind him.

If you ever look at the sky and see a cloud shaped like a boy, you'll know that it is Chang, for he still has not learned that kindness to others can bring one wealth.

KINDNESS TO OTHERS CAN BRING ONE WEALTH.

Story Sources

All the stories in this book are from the oral tradition, and similar tales can be found in many different countries. Here are some other versions of the stories that I have collected and retold in this volume:

"The Rooster and the Golden Button"
Kate Seredy tells a version of this story in her autobiographical novel *The Good Master*. For the hole in the Sultan's pocket, I owe special thanks to Fran Stallings, who has recorded her version on audio-cassette: *Storytelling with Autoharp* (Prairieflower Productions, 1991).

"Why the Beetle has a Gold Coat"
There is a version of this story in *South American Wonder Tales*, collected by Frances Carpenter (Follett, 1969). The paca is a member of the rodent family and looks somewhat like a large guinea pig.

"Maria and the Stingy Baker"
Stories of the Americas collected and translated by Frank Henius (Dodd, 1944).

"The Bird with Golden Feathers"
Lion Outwitted by Hare and Other African Tales, collected by Phyllis Savory (Albert Whitman, 1971).

"Rumpelstiltskin the Gold Spinner"
The Complete Grimm's Fairy Tales (Pantheon, 1944).
Special thanks to Ed Stivender, who suggested the Prince.

"King Midas and the Golden Touch"
It is thought-provoking to compare and contrast the Greek/Roman version of the story of Midas (as found in Rex Warner's *The Stories of the Greeks*, NY; Farrar, Straus & Giroux, 1967) with Nathaniel Hawthorne's richly descriptive version ("The Golden Touch" from *A Wonder Book for Girls and Boys*, by Nathaniel Hawthorne, reprinted in May Hill Arbuthnot's *The Arbuthnot Anthology of Children's Literature*, 4th ed., revised by Zena Sutherland, Scott Foresman, 1976.

"The Pumpkin Seeds"
Another version of this story is published in *Two Brothers and Their Magic Gourds*, ed. by Edward B. Adams, Seoul, Korea: Seoul International Tourist Publishing Co., 1981.

B.B.

Author's acknowledgements:
I would like to acknowledge the support of my storytelling colleagues – both in Patchwork, Philadelphia's Storytelling Guild and at the Free Library of Philadelphia – and to the children who have helped me "field-test" stories. Special thanks go to DianeJude McDowell, Special Collections Librarian, Central Children's Department, and to Larry Richards and the staff of the InterLibrary Loan Department, for helping me to locate rare, out-of-print and scholarly materials.

Dorling Kindersley would particularly like to thank the following people:
Natascha Biebow for editorial assistance, Clair Watson for design assistance, and Robert Graham for artist's reference.